AT HAJJ

Amaan Hyder was born in 1982. He is a graduate in English of University College London, and of the Creative Writing MA at the University of East Anglia. His poetry has appeared in various journals, including *Poetry Review*, *POEM* and *Blackbox Manifold*. *At Hajj* is his first collection.

At Hajj

Amaan Hyder

Penned in the Margins
LONDON

PUBLISHED BY PENNED IN THE MARGINS
Toynbee Studios, 28 Commercial Street, London E1 6AB
www.pennedinthemargins.co.uk

First published 2017

Printed in the United Kingdom by TJ International

ISBN
978-1-908058-44-7

CONTENTS

At Hajj

■

He sees people standing to pray, putting their hands on their knees and drawing up and going down to touch their foreheads to the ground. These are the movements his thoughts make. They sit for a while at the end of their prayers. They sit long after the prayers are over and ask what they have to ask for. You can walk between the groups and know they are all asking in silence. You can see that.

The Clot

Alif

What is a fit?
A holy thing is a fit.
A life is a fit.

I hear fifty machines stitching,
inking a grip.
Someone came to the door.

Someone was listening to us.
When I wake I am told what happened.
I pressed eject, mouths my father.

I pressed enough, mouths my mother.
She leaves in a car that shoots light.

Lam

What is a fit?
Someone trying to believe is a fit.
A life is a fit.

I'm sitting at the dining table.
I don't know what the words mean

but I know the letters. This is alif,

this is beh, this is the sword that
shoots light. Yes, that's right, I nod.
I can see my father in the hallway,

signing the channel to be recorded.
My father is a video forwarded.
My mother is a video recorded over.

Do you remember ejecting a tape,
the ribbon crackling behind it?
That's the currency.

A snippet of preface notes.
Someone making a face in belief is a fit.
One country and then another is a fit.

Mim

In America, there are Mayo and Baylor.
There is a video of opinion meeting itself.
They request you rewind as a courtesy.

So I'm sitting at the dining table.
I don't know what the words mean
but I know the letters. There is my father

interrogating after.
There is my mother and what's going on
behind our heads. There are the letters

passing through my fingers:
this is a house, this is an ox's head.
This is beh, this is alif.

Coats

My parents in a playground,
playing Follow The Leader.

I take my father aside. He says, 'My father says...'
I take my mother aside. She says, 'My father says...'

We walk through school, me between them,
their small hands reaching up to mine.

They are given messages to carry between classrooms.
The *rr* you get in squirrel is an English sound they don't have.

At lunchtime I see Mr Speedy take off his jumper.
His shirt rides up:

I come out to them.
They are looking to see who has eaten the mash.

Yesterday, when they were clearing their plates,
my father was scolded for accidentally dropping his cutlery in the
food bin.

'The light wasn't open,' they say.
Their drawings are pinned to a noticeboard.

They point out which houses are theirs.

I don't recognise them.

These are the pictures they grow up in.

■

The young man faces away from him, looking out to the crowds. He has finished his prayers and will be silent now while they are meant to be with their own thoughts. There is someone with a cough nearby. They have heard it a number of times. They look through the crowd to their right, past people praying and those talking, those getting up to find somewhere else to be, picking up their mats and shaking the sand off them.

On Arafat he needs to remember to eat or there is the risk he will become sick. He picks up the small bag by his feet and he takes out what is in there: a handful of dates and nuts wrapped a few times in cloth so he has to turn the package over and over until he can get to them. He picks out a date and puts it into his mouth and he takes another date and a few of the nuts. When he is eating the young man comes over and asks him whether he is feeling well and he nods. The young man has to bring his head right down to speak to him and he sits down at the old man's feet after he hears the answer.

At his shins, the pain is bad. Each time he puts down a foot, he has to take a breath. There is the heat also. The middle of the day makes the pain easier and means that he is able to walk more than he has been able to walk previously. When he started, when the walking began, he was shocked at how much he was managing. Each movement of the cane going forward, one more step than he had expected to make and no hoarse breathing. He was able to walk the whole first day and it was as if they said somewhere that the place for him was the desert but no one had told him and he had had to find out for himself and a man sitting in his childhood house in the forest knew nothing of all of this. That such a thing might be unknown.

The old man.

Mohammed's Mobile

I think Mohammed peace be upon him would have had one of those phones that aren't big or black like you sometimes get in old TV programmes. He wouldn't have had any pictures on the wallpaper because that would have been like eating pork but he might have had a tasbi on the top bit because you can get tasbis which slot into the hole where the headphones go.

The one I mean is the one Faraan my cousin has. I believe the colour of Mohammed's phone would have been white because that was the colour he liked to wear. I feel that he would have written his name on the back of his phone because he was a good man. He would have kept his phone clean and washed his hands before he used it. I am certain that he would have kept his phone switched off so that he would not disturb other people. His phone would have been on vibrate.

> Mohammed was a good man.
> He looked with big black eyes.
> He lived in different places
> and both his parents died.

> His wife was called Khadijah.
> She believed him first
> and then Ali was second.
> The Devil was the worst.

My brother's called Mohammed.
He's always in our room.
He's stopped watching TV
and he hates middle school.

My dad does not believe him
and neither does my aunt.
My mother would tell them
but she's in Pakistan.

To make my brother happy
we go out on our bikes.
We stay away from others,
eat Bountys in the night.

End of the Hall

apostrophes transform nouns
one's   two's   three's

bathwater   we skim stones
given names   uncollected

ours a waited English
you go in last   blackis

h end of the word
stepping into water

■

The young man has got him up to his feet, to his cane, and he has watched the young man throw stones for him. The young man has turned after throwing the stones as if he is his grandson looking back to see whether the stones have been thrown correctly. When there is a whole crowd throwing them, when the stones are colliding in the air, it's a sight.

It is only a moment of tiredness, he says to the young man. He tells the young man in his language and puts a hand on his cheek.

He decides to accompany the old man. The old man motions that he will wait and gives him his stones and tells him to throw them for him. He has all the stones in his hands now and he must throw for the two of them – the old man who could be his grandfather. He does not move into the crowd. He stands where he knows he can throw over the crowd in front of him. If he turns he knows he will see the old man. He turns after he throws the first two stones. He turns to the old man and sees him leaning hard on his stick. He throws the next two stones and he tries to follow them to the pillar but the stones are lost in the air and he turns to the old man before they land. The man's head is down and his eyes are raised. From a distance it is unclear what the man is looking at, whether he looks at him at all, at what he is doing. He throws the last stones. A man comes up to him and says to him in his language that he has thrown too many and the young man turns and points to the old man to explain himself. The old man has fallen over. He runs over to him and lifts him and the old man holds onto his arm and takes hold of his stick and he tries to sit the old man down but in his position it is more comfortable for him to lean on the cane. It is easier standing up. Sitting down, the man would be dependent on him completely.

Inheritable Landscape

I

Can I run round? Yes you can run round,
but Mohammed, can you come here?
Let me tell you where you can run round.

A pot handle. Or a cup handle
designed for if you don't want
to put your hand in the fire.

A ladder of buzzers.
This machine, I tell you.
He will not be your friend. Not at

but not unhappy.
I'm blinking out an eyelash.
Blinking out tourists is the taxi.

It's the Smoke. Late in the movement.
Citizens of carbohydrate,
hopeful connoisseurship.

Don't copy me. I'm a bad
crosser of roads, was an opener.
It was during a sculling lesson

on a lake the other side of town.
The instructor kept on turning
to X to ask my name.

Kept on using the spoon
that's been in the rice.
Don't pass it, he stared.

II

The unmentioned is
that I'm jake with everyone in this ballad.
I tried tracking them down last month

but it's odd they left on the assumption
the stats have aligned.
Sameer's grown, got his own

how's your bottom?
How do I not leave them, pocket-sore,
and get to you?

On the spine of a street: two bikes,
excited. Two at festivals.
You're going to look back and

I'm going to look back and
there's been this van up and down

past the shop really slow.

I'm excited to see our raspberries are
ready and they shouldn't be ready
for another month.

III

Why do I remember the original,
forget the eight bars of the harmonium?
Feroze pointed out that I never

slept with my arms by my sides, hands
collecting signatures across
the diaspora. Everywhere arthritis,

WhatsApp fallings out.
The interview began
as a conversation between

lust overcoming fear walking
in the house at night.
I emailed it to myself and forgot,

by nineteen, I knew the country was all —
have they called Y to menswear?
As if we're not busy?

Hence the garb. Hence the drag,
hence the dross.
We need to encourage people to join

the grassroots. Save announcements
of change, it has made a mockery of
all of us. And *apropos* plunges:

what's it like to soak in milk?
Do you open your eyes?
Do you see white? Do you

feel it in your bones?

Salaams

Where is this happy table from?
asked the old-fashioned at the bar.

The table coloured.
I followed him upstairs,

shed my happy hairs.
He went to his sock drawer for protection.

What do you think of these harlequin-pattern socks?
On the train, standing,

thinking it's the stop,
I thought not of grace.

Light dappling my toes.
When I was young there was a forest

shuffling shadows of men.
I would watch them with their backs to me.

■

Her leaving the crowd is faster. There are people like her wanting to find a space close to the pillar. As she moves she sees people saying their prayers, whispering to themselves. There are people shouting, there are people well behind the crowd who are running and throwing their stones as if they are throwing out to sea.

She carries the last stones in her hand and she moves forward. She holds her hands up to her face. There are people stretching their arms back, swinging their arms forward, throwing their stones at the pillars. She wants to get as close as possible to the front of the crowd. She holds up her arms by her face. She is hit by people's arms flung back. In order to move forward she has to lead with her shoulder as her arms are up by her head. She shoulders her way forward and she has to push hard. Between two figures she can't move forward any further. She watches them taking their time between stones. From behind, a hand hits her on her head, which knocks against her raised hands. She waits for the two figures in front of her to throw their remaining two stones. She watches as their hands pull back and she moves out of the way each time. They throw their stones one after the other. If she looks up she sees stones flying above her head. In front of her a stone falls short and lands in the crowd. Another time a stone hits the pillar at an odd angle and falls not far from her, in the crowd. There is the sound of stones hitting the pillar as she moves forward. The sound of the stones in the air like sparrows flying past. The figures in front of her have turned and walked out of the crowd and she has moved out of their way and uses the space they have left to move forward. She makes her way to the front. She has watched people as they have thrown their stones, as they have said their words and moved away. She has moved forward to where the stone landed that bounced off the pillar. She has wanted to get that close. She has looked about for other women and she has seen other women as far forward as this and she has stood still and when the time is right she throws her first stone. She pulls her arm back and she feels her hand grazing a cheek and she launches the stone into the air and she loses it. Above her two stones collide and find their way into the crowd. She cannot turn to see whose face she has grazed. The crowd is too strong here. An arm in front of her suddenly reaches back and she is hit on the nose. Her eyes well up. She puts her head down lower than the height of an arm swung back and puts her hand to her nose. She looks at her hand through her tears and wipes her eyes and sees the hand is the same colour it has been. She looks up. She moves back as a hand swings again. She raises her hand and throws the second stone. She turns as soon as she does it. The thwacks she hears are the stones off the pillar. Someone nearby is screaming as he throws. There are shouts as if there is someone approaching, someone in the distance to be called out to. She has now lost sight of the first stone and she has thrown the second without being able to look and she wants to see the third all the way to the pillar. A stone hits her uplifted hand. She puts her hand down and sees the graze. She does not put her hand to her mouth. She tenses her body, her legs. She pushes down to the ground and raises her arms and throws the stone and follows it as best she can and there is a sky full of stones so she can't follow an individual one. She follows what she thinks is it, which is a stone which is another stone which is another stone.

Hyderabad

The state tripped on its carpets last night,
has a black eye.

I can't see over the dashboard.
My client until I am six is my jailbird

father. I check invoices, frame scores.
When I'm gone from this country...

a molar sings. By your son it will be done.
He puts trunks through the mangle,

takes the excess west, ceiling drip to toilet —
so his bride is welcomed,

his mother on her shoulders. Rouge on
the capital distracts from the shiner.

Calling Mohammed

I. THE EARTH

The earth calls
to the universe.

Whatever is there behind this truck this wall
stay where they are.

II. THE EARTH SOAKED BY RAIN

I am Mohammed. In the morning we pray before sunrise. And we
pray after sunrise. And in the late afternoon. And after sunset. And
we pray in the night when it is completely dark.

I am Mohammed. This place is named after me, Mohammed's
Leap. Here is the bakery, the grocery. Here is the jeep at the end of
the street. There are the buildings. Here is the tallest, my namesake.

I am Mohammed. We could reduce the deposit to one month's
rental advance. Essentially my mother will have to pay, which
is the agreement. But last time I saw you were going to put him
on the spot a little bit. It's called the no effort way of farming —
no compromise, no middle ground. A father. Mine was a rocket
scientist. He had a brain tumour, died when he was fifty. He had
a nice little farm in the green forest. I don't think the legislature is

quite as forgiving there. He used it for two years and then gave it to me. To coin a phrase, you don't see

It is names across the street, flung back. It is names in work, names in schools, in windows shot with drink, fires. Tired notes, cut outs, with glue and paint and hovering above a chant.

My brother, Mo, is at dinner.
My brother, Mo, is with dominoes.

§

I. THE EARTH

The earth calls
to the universe.

Whatever is there behind this truck this wall
stay where they are.

II. THE EARTH SOAKED BY RAIN

'Call him,' Mum says
but not in English. 'Look at
what Dad did,' Aziza says,
pointing to the shadow on the carpet.

The sweat of his feet in his shoes, those are his feet in the wet earth. The earth soaked by rain, calling Mohammed. Whoever is outside when they come into the truck, when they climb over the partition they will land into a muddy bed. When they shine the torch, there will be a few plants, a few creepers beneath their feet, fruits burst, nothing but.

Dad puts his finger in front of the hose,
aims the jet —

they run screaming into the house.
Mo in linen, Mo in plastic, Mo on the slide

There will be a thud, there is a thud there by his head and he can see everyone. They are thinking to run to the door and run out as soon as it is opened, to leap out of the truck as far as they are able to and keep running. No, if this truck starts again I am going to run, I am going to open the door and run while it is moving. I'll jump into the street, into whatever is there behind this truck this wall and you will see my feet on the road.

They see it too, that long black body. The dragonfly.
They don't really like them but stay where they are.
Mohammed runs into the house, closes the patio door.

§

III. CALLING MOHAMMED

I am Mohammed watching Mohammed fall. I am Mohammed watching
Mohammed fall

My brother, Mo, is in his room.
My brother, Mo, is in school,

is when he is hugged,
is sweetly,

is talking, not talking,
is walking, not walking,

Mo mischievous

§

I. THE EARTH

Not Mohammed.
No, not Mohammed, but

The earth calls
to the universe.

Mo

§

Hello
It's me, Mo

Mo from the house
Mo in the night
Mo with permission
Mo about to speak

■

He walks back to the camp where his adopted group wait. They are sleeping or lying down or reading. When they see him they invite him to read with them. They raise the book to him but he turns away from them and lies down. They don't go up to him because they know he is not one of them and they can give him that privacy. There is chatter about him from others nearby. A tent next to him with a child crying loudly. He thinks on what he had done. He puts a hand to his shoulder which aches. He has put his shoulder through it and he finds it difficult to lie in a position that is comfortable. The crying in the tent nearby comes to a stop and he hears the wind between the tents. He thinks of the lost boy he had raised to his shoulders. He puts a hand up to the side of his neck and then across to his shoulder. It is rare not to hear the crowds, not to hear the voices going up and the replies coming down.

The old man goes in after a while − it is his turn. He can feel the swell of men at his arm, the swell of their languages. When the old man goes in, he does not need to put his arm down because it is pushed away and the men file in behind him. He steps away. He does not want to be here anymore.

He is the one who is closest to snapping now. There are men lining up at his arm, speaking their languages, pushing against his arm. They wait there against his arm because they can now see what he is doing or it has only been an arm that has been needed, an outstretched arm.

He needs the toilet and he joins the lines of men. He waits and waits and watches as people walk into the toilet without joining the back of the line.

Occasionally the line does move forward but he finds there are men who will take no notice of the older people in the line and will walk into the toilet as if the place was empty. After a while, as his line moves forward slowly, he decides that he will make it clear that no one will step in front of the old man in front of him. That man is three times his age at least. The man leans on a stick, his back is crooked and his face looks down to the floor. He walks by inches and not by steps. When the old man's turn is next, he puts his arms out and stops every man who tries to make his way before the old man. In order to do it he puts his arm against a wall and the men trying to push in front of them stand there, chests against his outstretched arm. He stands there and watches until it is the turn of the old man. The old man can't see what he is doing but he doesn't need the old man to know. He just needs to clear the way for him.

My father in his bed sounds like ice cracking

We're back to the days of treasure hunts,
dropping our bags and coats and comments

where we had sunk their predecessors so often.
We walk heavily up stairs,

looking for other motives.
The talk and tread

of kin above the drowsy bull who wades
in sleep and stands and walks amongst the blades

of grass he eats that calm his furry head.
We rise. He shakes his head at the order.

The house and its innards
over hot, steaming dishes.

Memory's a whittler. I've been thinking
what happens when we get to the pier.

Everything evanescence between
carousel and undertow.

I do not have time to sit by the fire with you,
Ice. Boys ask me to buy cigarettes.

I know they're out there, the shopkeeper said.
The first art I knew was learning how to breathe.

When I woke he was gone.
In the bathroom he had turned to water.

Water's a whittler.
There was a stretch where

I was uncontracted for six months;
then I got chow and oil and we drove,

memory delineated by hair.
It was a habit of mine to cut and fry.

One kid can ruin the class.

Wet Collected

Dancers stamp
Earth! Earth!

Coy Beau, not gym,
don't bury him in muscle.

The way of flightless birds.
Emerging first,

a drip diving hairs in a beard.
I swim in licks, sips,

blankets full of sticks,
damp mirrors, lube

and London.
Coy Daoud,

uncollected.
Assembling sprawl.

Dancers stamp
for their new king,

Earth! Great, raucous
habit of the eyes.

■

They approach a group of huts. He knows in the dream that someone in one of those huts is waiting for him and he does not know who it will be. Only that he is eager to follow the dog at a pace. Gauze over the dream.

They talk when they stop singing, and when they stop talking they sleep. They unroll a mat for him, one of their own, and he sleeps near them. He dreams the dog returns and is walking by his side and is running off in front of him.

The history they know is a history of movement, of fires put up when night falls and put out in the morning and dotted about the country the ashes trampled on and forgotten and carried for whatever reason. Something to carry in one's hand and let fall to the ground.

He walks in this way for the rest of the day, gauze against the light. He meets a caravan and two men walk up to him, their hands at their side because he has come out of nowhere. Behind them the dog runs up to him and puts its paws up on his leg and when he goes down onto his knees it's a sign to the men that he is no one to be concerned about. He joins the caravan and he drinks and eats when it is dark. The people make a fire and they tell stories and sing and draw closer to each other and to the fire.

There is the heat beating down on him. He stands and pulls his robe down over his eyes and opens his eyes and presses the robe to his face and he can see through the robe then. He can see the landscape made black by the robe. He can see through the light to the mountain behind. A breeze has started, has lessened the strength of the sun.

There is a shadow of water up ahead. The dog runs off suddenly. A burst of energy from somewhere and he calls out to him to stop but the dog has seen something. He is alone. When he looks up, his eyes are blinded and he cannot see what is coming towards him. He looks up and brings his robe down over his eyes and he shuts his eyes and sees the light turned red there. And he stops and doesn't open his eyes again for a while. He continues walking and he stops. He cannot walk blind. He won't be able to see the mountain in the distance that he has been using to mark his place. He drops to his knees. He puts his hands around his eyes and he sees black.

As he walks, he puts his robe over his head and the part of the robe that dangles from his shoulder he puts over the head of the dog so the dog has some shade while they are walking. It's a game for the dog. The heat builds and builds and he sees the huts again but he cannot get close to them.

The man asks him where he is going while they watch the dog drinking from the bucket and he tells the man. The man says farewell to him and looks away to the direction he is headed. He can't tell whether the man thinks his way is safe or not. The man turns his face and watches the dog finish drinking from the bucket. When the dog looks up to him, he thanks the man and he and the dog leave the collection of huts and continue walking in the desert heat.

He nears a group of huts. As he approaches, a man comes out of one of the huts and waits for him and he walks forward and the dog looks up at him and he looks down at the dog. He looks back to the man and asks him if he has any water and the man walks him to one of the huts where the dog drinks water out of the bucket.

In the night he puts down what he has collected and he makes a fire and he pulls his robe over himself and whatever it is that has been following him he lets watch over him for those hours he is asleep. When he wakes he sees a dog on the other side of the glowing embers. The dog lies with its head down between its paws and its eyes open and he knows dogs enough, he has owned dogs himself enough, to know that it is a trick the dog has learned. Someone has told the dog to wait there. When he gets up he stretches, his back hard and cold, and he wipes the sweat from himself and puts a hand to his side where a flask of water might be but he remembers there is nothing there. He is without any sustenance. He puts a tongue to his cracked lips and he tastes salt and he wipes his eyes and he walks on. He turns and the dog is standing by the embers and he taps his hand twice on his thigh and the dog runs over to him. As he walks, if he stretches out his fingers he feels the dog's head and occasionally the wet of its tongue or its nose.

He wonders whether there was something following him. He walks and he turns whenever he hears a noise, something running off behind him. There is nothing there but where he has come from and his own footprints leaving a trail. He tells himself stories as he walks. He tells himself what is going to happen, what he is going to do for himself and for others.

Grain

We will look back on our time
as ruined lives and think doing
good work will bear some reward,
but it gives only false impression.

As ruined lives and think doing,
such are the journeys we make.
But it gives only false impression.
We will think less of the world,

such are the journeys. We make
neat bites on cobs, animal sounds.
We will think less. Of the world,
I suggest remembering lines of code:

'neat bites on cobs', 'animal sounds'.
We will look back on our time,
I suggest, remembering lines of code.
Good work will bear some reward.

■

He had been in his own group, walking in a line with his hands around the waist of the man in front. His group had been snaking through the crowds like that for a few days. One morning he had been at the back of the line and he had felt the crowds closing in. He had not seen it bottleneck so badly before. The message went down the line to hold on tight and he had the sweat of the man in front on his beard.

Next to him a boy fell to his knees and he let go and helped the boy to his feet. The boy began to cry and he panicked and lifted him onto his shoulders and shouted as loud as he could in his language that the boy was lost. He yelled and the boy cried. He didn't know what to do. His group couldn't stop for him. A little while later the boy saw a familiar and scrambled into the hands of the pilgrims in between. He watched him go. It was over like that.

I've seen him asking around for his people, that man. The orphan. He had been in his own group, walking in a line with his hands around the waist of the man in front. He says in his language that he is lost. And watches while the message he sends out goes down the line like a boy scrambling on shoulders in a crowd. The scent bottlenecks at his beard and in his sleep he is lost and lifted and let go in the cried-out desert.

two urines

in the desert of night
note cold houses & the thought of men
whose pish i replenish

lunk leaves gold unflushed
habit of a boys' dormitory
in which he grew eating poorly

cooked fish nobody
teaching him to cross
not to piss in

the street
enamoured &
by increments

mug clanging confidence
who doesn't itch watching this
i bake shiver

less
stretched mouth
rung as a city block

fried flower
on absorbent cloth

aria's arc

no subtle art
in length and sound
envy and clown

At Dinner

It's something our grandparents, our grandfathers, used to do without question, and so no one, not one member of our fathers' generation did, and now I'm doing it — that's the irony. I expect the generation below us, our children, won't, that they will be the staunchest critics, as my father and mother were. I suppose things proceed in this way. What is an orthodoxy with one generation, generally, is thrown off by the next and so on. Now, really, it's religion more than smoking. Although that seems to occur every two generations rather than one. You must have heard the same from your mother and father, I think; that the parents of our grandparents were religious people, were strict — well, so my mother and father used to tell me — and because of that our parents and our own generation aren't so religious. And now the generation below us, those coming up, our children even, for them religion has come to be something important again. It's hard to say though whether this is indeed a recurrence, just a reaction to the reaction, or whether it is stirred up in the first place by something outside the pattern I have described, whether it follows the trend of foreign policy, or indeed whether it is due to both of these patterns colliding — perhaps that is why the sentiment is particularly strong in so many young people now, where it wasn't at all in us. Where it had skipped us, or us it.

Cement

Dreams going round like hot food in a mouth.
You get old here quicker than in the south.
Or you don't. A bite without flesh, the years
without movement, that is Ghost City. Night
after night you can christen every floor
of Sun Mall. It's like having a whore,
village boy, in the middle of a field.
No cows to watch. Sleep is fossilized tears.
Dust the regional flavour. If they peeled
your skin, they would find it like grit in meal
or gold in mud, your cough the hopeless sieve.
At work it doesn't matter how you feel;
when you spit just aim for somewhere not white.
Managing blood is knowing how to live.

■

In the tent, the first man returned to his bed after going to the toilet and found an impostor, someone he had never seen before, sleeping in his bed. When the impostor woke up because of the noise the first man was making, the impostor said he would only be asleep for a while, a couple of hours, seven hours at the most (he was unable to sleep any longer than seven hours), and the first man could wait until then couldn't he? Surely he could wait until he had finished, until he had rested — the man had so much energy, one could tell from the way he was speaking, the way he had gathered a crowd about him, men and women, each getting a word in. Lord, did any of them even need to sleep at that time?

Sleeves

The sleeves of the coat Anees gave me are too long and they rub against the back of my hands and my skin has become dry and red there. I've tried folding them back but two things happen: one is that the inside, the lining, shows; and two is that they never stay but they slowly unfold. I thought I should stitch the sleeves after folding them inwards or cutting them, but I don't want to cut them because when Anees bought the coat I put it on in front of him and I put my hands behind my back so he didn't see the sleeves and his feelings were saved. (And what would I say to him if he saw me with a cut coat?)

I met a man in the lift with a long green coat and I folded my sleeves back twice and he took a safety pin out of his pocket and offered it to me. He pulled his trouser leg up above the knee and said his trousers were pinned but I couldn't see, so I put my hand underneath and I could feel the beat in his leg. He lived two floors up so he remained in the lift after and I thought the lift is the inside sleeve of the building. It is black and when the doors open heat escapes.

The sleeves of the coat are the right length now because I have pinned them and the holes don't show because they are too small (I can remove the pins before Anees sees me and he will never have to know). I wear the long green coat too by putting my hands into the inside sleeves or I smooth them up the leg and the coat rests on my shoulders in folds like edges of a hood, or I put my hands in the pockets with his and our fingers overlapping go in and press and circle and out like zigzags snug-tight hot and the heat is another layer around us too.

Kamal's Baba's Head

Kamal's Baba's head is a bottle inverted,
titled,
about to be taken down.

Kamal's Baba hit his own twin brother round the head with a lamp when they were twenty years old and then his twin brother had a brain operation. Kamal's Baba's twin brother died after the operation but Kamal told me the swinging lamp and the brain operation weren't connected. Kamal's Baba got married quite soon after that and then Kamal was born some years later. I was born on the same day as Kamal, but two years after. When we were still very young our parents used to throw a single party for the two of us like we were twin brothers. The photos we have in our albums show that it happened more than once, so, I suppose, Kamal's Baba had forgotten about other twins and brothers.

Once I went round to Kamal's house after not seeing him or his Baba or his Ma for a long time. Kamal and his Ma were not in but Kamal's Baba had come down from upstairs to open the door. He said that he had been reading a book in Kamal's room and would I like to come upstairs.

Kamal's Baba's head is a bottle inverted,
titled,
about to be taken down.

On Kamal's desk were two magazines, a desk-lamp, and a toy figurine of a policeman in the corner. The policeman was a present that my parents gave Kamal on our fourth and sixth birthday and I remember Kamal tying tape round the policeman's neck so the policeman could swing from upstairs to downstairs in a whiz and Kamal could hold the hoop of tape. Kamal's Baba told me they had arranged a video call with Kamal. There was a noise, soldiers running behind Kamal, and the call was stopped. You know, when there's movement the head comes off, Kamal's Baba said. First I though he was talking about his brother and lamp. I thought of a man still like a bottle smashed on a table in a room. Kamal's Baba got up from the bed and the policeman dropped and rolled to the end of the desk.

Kamal's Baba's head is a bottle inverted,
titled,
about to be taken down.

■

PerpetualTawaf.com and MallTawaf.com had twenty-four hour footage of the insiders. You could follow Zainab #21 on your computer by selecting her profile. During the regular Hajj those people who were physically unable in some way, those who had a bad leg, or who needed all their energy to take a step, said the sheer occasion allowed them to do it. Some onlookers believed that such a spirit was in the mall now, guiding the insiders round, giving them the energy. Yes, and some had their servants carry them the whole Hajj. There was no ghost in the mall but corporate spectre. Had anyone, in fact, tested the air in the place? What drug was being pumped into the air preventing these poor people from leaving? Stones were hurled through a few of the mall's windows: people waited for the blur of fumes. None of the Hajjis were hurt — the stones were left where they fell. Some advocated for a stronger militarized attack. There had been a few people, a few policemen, and later twenty soldiers had been dispatched. The soldiers, the policemen, those attempting to 'rescue' their loved ones, ended up in the same position as those on the inside. No difference between the people and stones. When the cameras at the windows zoomed into a face each individual looked unperturbed. A soldier in fatigues smiled back. Zainab #21 waved at the drone.

What Were Giraffes?

Remember horses? They were like horses
but a great deal taller, with a tough skin
patterned like baked earth and a strong, long, thin
neck which meant they could not run like horses
but had to bob their necks back and forth to
keep balance while they hurried anywhere.
They had thick eyelashes, Mohawk mane hair,
ate from the highest branches, and had to
spread their front legs to reach down to the earth,
each having fallen two metres at birth.
Lengthy quirks like these made giraffes comic
gold in cartoons and movies — the slapstick
beasts of choice, best bang for your buck laughs
on an African plain. Those were giraffes.

At Dinner

Towards the end of the meal, when our dessert was served — it was an Asian dessert, one I had eaten a number of times, a lozenge-shaped slice of condensed milk and yoghurt, steamed and hardened into something a little stiffer than a mousse, and then topped with two raspberries in the European tradition of garnishing desserts. And beneath the fruit, on top of the diamond of the dessert, were flakes of edible silver, or edible foil. The edible silver that so often garnishes the surface of South Asian desserts in restaurants. I remember separating off a piece of the stuff with my teaspoon; a flake of the silver with the white of the dessert underneath. I have never prepared a dessert with that foil but I know from what I have seen on television that it acts as an adhesive, sticking to most surfaces it comes into contact with, breaking into pieces if one tries to handle it. That's why, when it is used by chefs, it is always peeled away from its wrapper with small tweezers, the kind of instrument used by archivists or archaeologists when handling minute artefacts, turning delicate pages, lifting up small grains or stones, placing them on a dish and sliding them under the lens of a microscope.

■

What she knows very keenly now is the pain in her shoulder. She moves into a space and brings her supporting arm down and her good arm up to the woman she has been leading. They are through it now. The woman has her head turned; she is looking for her people. The woman takes a few steps away from her.

A gap appears ahead of her, a brief sight over the pilgrims in front. It is some space, a break. Because people are slowing down, she has practically come to a stop, but there is a push from the back. The crowd wants to move forward, move through. For a moment she is off the ground; she and the woman are off the ground and put back down a moment later. She feels it in her shoulder. She hears the woman's voice. That drive was the last of the bottleneck.

She is aching at her sides up from her waist and she needs to sit down, but that could be the best way of not building up stamina. What she needs to do is keep going. They are at the end of the bottleneck now, they are hardly moving forward. Just inching forward, pressed together. She cannot see her feet. She can hardly turn to see the old woman. Their linked arms are dangerous now were there to be a movement hard in any direction. Their arms can only take so much weight.

They are in the middle of the bottleneck. Her free arm glued to her side. There are lines of people with arms round each other as she is walking and they don't break, they don't make way for anyone getting through. She has to stop for a line coming through. They do not look at her. They do not look at the woman she leads or the woman's people. She turns back occasionally to see where they are. If she is lost she doesn't want others to be lost either. They are moving steadily behind her. They have kept their place. She couldn't place them, these people. She can't place where they are from. They are white, red in the sun. She turns and looks forward. She looks to where she is going and again there is the scratch on her cheek from a man's beard. She is not able to get her free hand up to her cheek.

They are moving through a bottleneck. She can see where it closes and beyond that she thinks she can see where there is more space, where people have more space between them.

She can only just see over the top of the crowd. There is a hand on her back. A hand on her shoulder, another down by her waist. As she gets to the worst part of the bottleneck a woman next to her starts speaking to her in her language. She shakes her head, doesn't understand. The woman is older than her, puts her hand on her shoulder. She needs to give her some support, this is what the woman wants she thinks, to get through the bottleneck. She is looking down at the woman. The woman can't see what she sees, the space further up ahead. She is able, in the little space she has, to raise a hand and put it on the woman's arm for support, so the two of them are linking arms. Occasionally one part of the crowd moving forward will pause and the other side will push forward so those in the middle, where they are, the two of them, will be twisted, turned, and will have to push back to right themselves. The old woman is worried about that happening again, she thinks. Half the trick is to stand behind a large person, someone who has some weight. There is some safety in that. There is a bit of danger too, if the man was to fall, or if the man was to twist round himself and lose his footing. No, the trick is to stay on one's feet, not to be lifted through the crowd in the bottleneck.

Next to the old woman are her people and they are as old as her, each of them leaning on another. She sees them all, a group. There again is a cheek against her cheek. A beard against her cheek. There is the smell of bodies in the sun and clothes full of sweat. Her shoulder is aching already, the woman is putting her weight on her and they are at an odd angle, the woman having fallen back behind her and she herself having moved forward.

As she was. She had lost the group. She had stopped to help someone and had got lost in turn. They had been told not to let go, not to separate themselves even to help someone. She is lost now. She moves forward in the stream of people, the stream of pilgrims.

There are some people carrying children in their arms, or else holding onto others, onto older people who are having trouble walking and need to stop every so often. There are people walking with their arms wrapped around the waist of the person in front of them. People walking in a line like that.

Some Permanence

Road markings are being repainted.
Did you know they prepare the surface of the road
by blasting the old markings with fire to fade them?

The first man comes along,
gas canister on his back, spout of fire in his hand,
and goes to each marking, blasting

fire onto the strip from top to bottom
until it has faded.
After him, the second man comes along,

pours fresh white paint from a jug into a contraption
that spreads the colour over the faded area.
The white looks very bright,

I think because the paint has something
which catches, glows, under the street light.
The man with the gas canister goes to the truck

(every truck that passes I think — is it that truck?)
and puts the canister in the back
next to the other canisters. The truck says,

Sign Painting. Says,
Government.

The second man continues with the overlaying.

It is just this stretch of road they are doing,
between the buildings.
They are old hands, perhaps.

It is something that does not take long to do in itself,
perhaps. The fire. The paint.
The new paint over the top of the faded,

burned-away markings beneath.
We watch from either side of the road, at a height.
We are itching to do it, the spout of fire

in our hands, the jug of paint —
who wouldn't be itching, watching this?
Thinking they can do it. Wanting to do it.

It seems like it would be rewarding,
making fade, pristine,
in a stroke.

We watch the second man as he finishes
what he needs to do.
We withdraw, hear the truck drive off —

the men, the canisters, the contraption
we did not know the name of.
What if we were to run down the stairs of the building,

sink our hands into the white?
It would be —
although the paint is probably quick to dry.

By the time we would have made it,
it would have dried, nothing left to repurpose.
A child on the terrace,

milking a laugh.
Sleep tempting
those on the benches.

Where would we be then?
We can only admit memories.
White. Of the frozen street,

there's nothing left to smudge.
The seasons before us,
their writing and our watching

intently. The language of
our replacements
everywhere and hard to reach.